Christian Heroes: Then & Now

CORRIE TEN BOOM

Unit Study

Curriculum Guide

JANET & GEOFF BENGE

AF584694

PUBLISHING

A Ministry Of Youth With A Mission

P.O. Box 55787, Seattle, WA 98155

YWAM Publishing is the publishing ministry of Youth With A Mission. Youth With A Mission (YWAM) is an international missionary organization of Christians from many denominations dedicated to presenting Jesus Christ to this generation. To this end, YWAM has focused its efforts in three main areas: 1) Training and equipping believers for their part in fulfilling the Great Commission (Matthew 28:19). 2) Personal evangelism. 3) Mercy ministry (medical and relief work).

For a free catalog of books and materials write or call:
YWAM Publishing
P.O. Box 55787, Seattle, WA 98155
(425) 771-1153 or (800) 922-2143
www.ywampublishing.com

Corrie ten Boom: A Unit Study Curriculum Guide
Copyright © 2001 by YWAM Publishing

10 09 08 07 06 05 04 03 02 01   10 9 8 7 6 5 4 3 2 1

Published by Youth With A Mission Publishing
P.O. Box 55787
Seattle, WA 98155

ISBN 1-57658-201-9

Verses marked KJV are taken from the King James Version of the Bible.
Verses marked NIV are taken from the Holy Bible, New International Version®, Copyright© 1973, 1978, 1984 by the International Bible Society. Used by permission of Zondervan Publishing House.
Verses marked RSV are taken from the Revised Standard Version of the Bible, Copyright 1946, 1952, 1971 by the Division of Christian Education of the National Council of the Churches of Christ in the U.S.A. Used by permission.

All rights reserved. No part of this book may be reproduced in any form without permission from the publisher. Permission is granted to the individual purchaser to reproduce student materials in this book for non-commercial individual or classroom use only. Permission is not granted for schoolwide reproduction of such materials.

Printed in the United States of America.

Contents

CORRIE TEN BOOM

1892–1983

Corrie ten Boom: A Unit Study Curriculum Guide

This unit study guide is designed to accompany the book *Corrie ten Boom: Keeper of the Angels' Den* from the Christian Heroes: Then & Now series by Janet and Geoff Benge. It provides the Christian school teacher and homeschooling parent with ways to use the book as a vehicle for teaching or reinforcing various curriculum areas, including

- Creative writing.
- Drama.
- Movie critiquing.
- Reading comprehension.
- Essay writing.
- History and geography concepts.

As there are more ideas than could possibly be used in one unit, it is the parent/teacher's job to sift through the ideas and select those that best fit the needs of the students.

Corrie ten Boom lived through the reign of Hitler and the Nazis in World War II. The annihilation of eleven million people—six million Jews and five million others—is a horrific and depressing part of history. *Teachers need to carefully review all materials for this unit, keeping in mind each student and the effect some of these materials, which are both graphic and disturbing, may have on him or her.* As a rule, do not expose a child to any more horror than is necessary to get across the point you are trying to make.

The activities recommended in this unit study guide are

- Reflective of a wide range of learning styles.
- Designed for both group and individual study.
- Suitable for a range of grade levels and abilities.

Learning Styles

Choose those activities that are best suited to your student or students. For example, when studying the physical features of a country, a kinesthetic learner will learn best by producing a three-dimensional clay model representing the physical features of the country, whereas a visual learner will find it more meaningful to produce a poster map of the country for the classroom wall.

Group or Individual Study

While the activities contained in this unit study guide are designed to be carried out by a student working alone, instructions are also provided for adapting an activity for a group.

Grade Levels/Abilities

As you thumb through this unit study guide, you will note that grade levels are not assigned to particular activities, though some areas, essay topics for example, progress from the simple to the complex. This approach has been taken because students of varying grade levels can undertake most of the activities. For example, one activity calls for students to write a poem based on black-and-white photos of bombed-out Rotterdam. A fourth grader doing this activity would tend to comment on the concrete objects he or she sees in the photos, such as crumbled buildings, dazed children, and broken water pipes. In contrast, a ninth grader undertaking the same assignment would be able to explore more abstract concepts, such as the emotions of the people in the photos and how the destruction of Rotterdam set the stage for the much more devastating destruction of Dutch society itself by the Nazis. Each student uses the same activity and instructions to create work appropriate to his or her age and cognitive ability.

In the center of this unit study guide you will find two foldout pages. These pages contain three maps and a fact sheet to be filled out by the student. The maps and fact sheet are designed to be photocopied onto individual pages so that each student can store them in his or her folder. They are for use with the social studies section of this unit study guide (chapter 6).

Before you begin teaching from this unit study guide, please read through each section. You may wish to highlight the activities that appeal to you or that you know your students would enjoy or be challenged by. Many teachers find it useful to plan the culminating event (see chapter 8) first and then select a range of learning activities that lend themselves to this event.

For the sake of brevity in the instructions that accompany each section, the word *teacher* includes the homeschooling parent, and the word *student* refers to a child either in a traditional classroom or in a home-school environment.

1

Key Bible Verses

The authors have selected four Bible verses that can be used alongside or as part of this unit study. For your convenience, these verses have been quoted in two versions: the King James Version and the New International Version. Of course, many other appropriate Bible verses can be added to the list if more are needed. The verses can be used in a number of ways. Four ideas for using them are listed below.

Memorization. The teacher can assign one or all of the verses to be memorized during the duration of the study. A chart could be made to track which students have completed memorizing which verses.

Meaning. The verses can be used to spark conversations on the spiritual aspects of Corrie's life. This can then be translated into action by having students form groups and present one of the verses to the class in a creative manner. Students could make up a skit to illustrate the meaning of the verse or present a one-act play to show how the verse was relevant in the life of Corrie ten Boom.

Devotional. The teacher might consider beginning a class or family devotional book. To do this, the teacher should familiarize the students with a variety of devotional writings and then ask them to write a devotion based upon their own understanding of one of the verses as it relates to the life of Corrie ten Boom. The pages could then be glued or copied into a blank book, illustrated, and signed. The various devotions could be read aloud at appropriate times, including during assemblies and family devotional times and at the culminating event.

Display. Students could design a plaque, wall hanging, poster, or banner with one of the verses written on it. This could be hung in a prominent place while the unit study is being undertaken and used for decoration during the culminating event.

"Thou art my hiding place and my shield: I hope in thy word." (Psalm 119:114 KJV)

"You are my refuge and my shield; I have put my hope in your word." (Psalm 119:114 NIV)

"But I say unto you, Love your enemies, bless them that curse you, do good to them that hate you, and pray for them which despitefully use you, and persecute you; That ye may be the children of your Father which is in heaven: for he maketh his sun to rise on the evil and on the good, and sendeth rain on the just and on the unjust. For if ye love them which love you, what reward have ye?" (Matthew 5:44–46 KJV)

“But I tell you: Love your enemies and pray for those who persecute you, that you may be sons of your Father in heaven. He causes his sun to rise on the evil and the good, and sends rain on the righteous and the unrighteous. If you love those who love you, what reward will you get?” (Matthew 5:44–46 NIV)

“See that none render evil for evil unto any man; but ever follow that which is good, both among yourselves, and to all men.” (1 Thessalonians 5:15 KJV)

“Make sure that nobody pays back wrong for wrong, but always try to be kind to each other and to everyone else.” (1 Thessalonians 5:15 NIV)

“Hereby perceive we the love of God, because he laid down his life for us: and we ought to lay down our lives for the brethren. But whoso hath this world’s good, and seeth his brother have need, and shutteth up his bowels of compassion from him, how dwelleth the love of God in him? My little children, let us not love in word, neither in tongue; but in deed and in truth.” (1 John 3:16–18 KJV)

“This is how we know what love is: Jesus Christ laid down his life for us. And we ought to lay down our lives for our brothers. If anyone has material possessions and sees his brother in need but has no pity on him, how can the love of God be in him? Dear children, let us not love with words or tongue but with actions and in truth.” (1 John 3:16–18 NIV)

2

Display Corner

Many students will enjoy collecting and displaying objects related to the places or events they are studying. It is motivational to designate a corner of the room, including a table or desk and wall space, that can be used for this purpose. Keep some index cards on the table and encourage students to label their contributions, including as much information as possible about where each object came from, what it is used for, and who would use it.

Encourage students to ask their parents and friends if they have anything interesting (but not valuable) related to the Netherlands, the Holocaust, or World War II in general. You could also visit your local library to find books on these topics or go to the websites listed in Appendix A to access numerous interesting maps, posters, leaflets, and other materials related to the topics. Following is a list of things students (or you) might like to display. Of course, there are many more options.

- A large map of Europe.
- Dutch food and food-related items, including chocolates, tea, teapots, teacups, and cookbooks.
- Potted tulip plants.
- Examples of Dutch writing, including Bibles and tracts. These are available through the American Bible Society at (800) 32-BIBLE or online at www.americanbible.org.
- Photographs and articles about the Netherlands, the Holocaust, or World War II, both from the past and the present.
- Newspaper articles about the Netherlands highlighting current events in the various regions of the country. (Note articles about how Jewish families have had to fight to recover their money from Swiss banks and about reparations many German companies have agreed to pay Nazi work camp internees.)
- Dutch stamps and coins.
- Dolls in native Dutch costume.
- Copies of the many books written by Corrie ten Boom.
- A replica of the parcel that the nurse gave Corrie (see *Corrie ten Boom: Keeper of the Angels' Den,* pages 109–111).
- A child's coat with a yellow Star of David patch sewn onto it.
- An old bicycle wheel wrapped in rags in place of the usual rubber tire.

3

Chapter Questions

There are four questions related to each chapter of *Corrie ten Boom: Keeper of the Angels' Den:*

1. A vocabulary question drawn from the text and referenced to a page in the book.
2. A factual question arising from the text.
3. A question to gauge the level of a student's comprehension.
4. An open-ended question seeking an opinion or interpretation.

These questions are designed for students to complete on their own. They are best answered as a student finishes reading each chapter in the book. Answers to the first three questions for each chapter are given in Appendix B. The answer to the fourth question is open-ended and needs to be evaluated separately. Since question four deals with a student's interpretation or opinions, it is a good question on which to base a group discussion. Keep in mind that there is no right or wrong answer to question four, just positions a student needs to justify.

To gain maximum benefit from the questions, the students should write full-sentence answers and not just one or two words. For example, in response to the question "What was the name of the young apprentice Corrie's father employed?" they should write, "The young apprentice's name was Jop" rather than just "Jop."

Each vocabulary question asks the students to use the new word in a sentence. If you ask them to do this, make sure their sentences clearly demonstrate the meaning of the vocabulary word.

As a supplement to answering the questions, you may ask the students to write a short summary of each chapter or write a response to the chapter in their journals. This could involve the students writing about how they relate to Corrie's actions, noting how they think they would react in a similar situation, and speculating as to what they think might happen next in the story.

Chapter One

1. What is a curfew (page 11)? Use the word in a sentence.
2. Where did the Gestapo take Corrie and her family?
3. What was Corrie worried about the Gestapo finding out?
4. Casper ten Boom was given the choice of stopping his aid to the Jews or staying in custody. What was his decision, and what does that tell you about his character?

Chapter Two

1. What is a disorder (page 21)? Use the word in a sentence.

2. What was really wrong with Corrie when she spent more than five months in bed?
3. Why did Corrie decide to become a watchmaker?
4. What qualities do you think Corrie must have had to found the Triangle Club? Explain your answer.

Chapter Three

1. What does assurance mean (page 36)? Use the word in a sentence.
2. How many radios did the Ten Booms have at the Beje before the war?
3. Why did Peter think the stairway outside his grandfather's room would be a good place to hide a radio?
4. Corrie told the Gestapo officer collecting the radios that they had only one at the Beje. Do you think she was justified in telling a lie? Why or why not?

Chapter Four

1. What are allies (page 50)? Use the word in a sentence.
2. What did the Germans require all Jews to wear on the front of their clothes when out in public?
3. How did Willem suggest Corrie solve the problem of not having enough food to feed the Jewish guests at the Beje?
4. Corrie's nephew Peter played "Wilhelmus," the Dutch national anthem, on the church organ, and Corrie's father began to sing it. Why do you think they risked their freedom to do this, and how do you think it made them and those around them feel?

Chapter Five

1. What is a cantor (page 64)? Use the word in a sentence.
2. What type of transport did Corrie use to get around Haarlem?
3. Why did Mr. Smit think the Beje was an ideal house in which to make a secret room?
4. Describe how you might feel if you knew you could be awakened at any time of the night and given sixty seconds to hide yourself and everything you own from the Gestapo.

Chapter Six

1. What is a dynamo (page 73)? Use the word in a sentence.
2. What did Eusie do to make the window washer think the people at the Beje were having a party?
3. Why did Corrie let Jop leave the Beje?
4. Do you think Corrie did the right thing in letting Jop leave the Beje? Why or why not?

Chapter Seven

1. What does defiantly mean (page 94)? Use the word in a sentence.
2. What punishment did Corrie's nephew Peter receive for playing the national anthem in church?
3. Why was the Gestapo officer delighted when there was a knock at the Beje door?
4. Of all the people captured in the raid on the Beje, who do you think would be in the most serious trouble with the Nazis? Why?

Chapter Eight

1. What does recoiled mean (page 103)? Use the word in a sentence.
2. What personal belongings did Corrie drop into the manila envelope?
3. Why was the young baroness in Corrie's cell in prison?
4. What were some of the things that would have burdened Corrie's mind as she lay in the cell? What do you think her father would have told her if he had been there with her?

Chapter Nine

1. What is pleurisy (page 109)? Use the word in a sentence.
2. What was in the package the nurse gave Corrie?
3. Why were the prisoners able to yell messages to one another?
4. Why do you think the doctor said, "I hope I have done you a favor reporting your pleurisy"?

Chapter Ten

1. What does defective mean (page 124)? Use the word in a sentence.
2. Who interviewed Corrie about her involvement with the underground?
3. How did the person who interviewed Corrie try to get her to tell him what she knew?
4. What effect do you think Corrie's words may have had on her interviewer? What makes you think so?

Chapter Eleven

1. What is an emblem (page 139)? Use the word in a sentence.
2. What was the name of the new camp Corrie and Betsie were taken to?
3. From where did the prisoners get their information about the progress of the war?
4. What effect do you think all of the rumors about being freed soon would have had on the prisoners? Do you think it would have been better for them to know or not know what would happen next? Why?

Chapter Twelve

1. What does auburn mean (page 153)? Use the word in a sentence.
2. How many women were forced into each boxcar?
3. Why were seven teenage boys able to control more than one thousand women?
4. What do you think made Corrie keep walking into the concentration camp when part of her wanted to lie down and die? Explain your answer.

Chapter Thirteen

1. What does clamored mean (page 163)? Use the word in a sentence.
2. What was the name of the factory where Corrie and Betsie worked?
3. Why was Corrie thankful for the fleas in her barracks?
4. Describe some of the things you think might have been running through Corrie's mind as she walked out the gates of Ravensbruck.

Chapter Fourteen

1. What does scrawny mean (page 174)? Use the word in a sentence.
2. How did Corrie get from Willem's house to Haarlem?
3. Why didn't Nurse Benes recognize Corrie?
4. Corrie took a risk in traveling on the food truck to Hilversum. Why do you think she took the risk? Do you think she made a wise choice? Explain your answer.

Chapter Fifteen

1. What does palatial mean (page 185)? Use the word in a sentence.
2. How many countries did Corrie visit after the war?
3. Why did Corrie refuse to have schedules and bells at the de Haan house?
4. How did allowing members of the NSB to live in the Beje honor Mr. Ten Boom? How do you think the neighbors might have reacted to NSB members moving in?

4

Student Explorations

Student explorations are a variety of activities that are appropriate to a wide range of learning styles. These activities consist of the following:

Essay Questions. These are questions that can be used as essay writing ideas. Students can either be assigned a topic or choose their own from the list. The simplest essay topics appear first, followed in order by those that are more complex.

Creative Writing. This includes writing such things as newspaper articles, poems, letters, resumés, songs, and journals.

Hands-On Projects. These are various kinds of projects, such as charts and graphs, models, comic strips, family crests, mottoes, dioramas, book covers, and mobiles.

Audio/Visual Projects. These involve such things as using a tape recorder to conduct a mock interview or to produce a radio play or commercial, or using still and video cameras to create dramatic presentations.

Arts and Crafts. These include art forms and crafts related to Corrie ten Boom's life.

Language Examples. Some examples of sentences written in the Dutch language are given. Students can use them to make banners or place mats for the culminating event, or in their hands-on projects. For example, they could use them around the edge of the Ten Boom family crest.

[Note on group projects: All the suggestions described below are individual learning activities. However, some of the activities have bracketed paragraphs like this one after them that offer suggestions on how the activity can be adapted for class or group use.]

Essay Questions

1. Watch one of the movies listed in the Related Movies and Documentaries section of Appendix A. Write about the similarities and differences between the experiences of the main character in the movie and Corrie ten Boom.

2. Albert Einstein wrote, "The world is a dangerous place to live—not because of the people who are evil, but because of the people who do not do anything about it." Write an essay explaining why you think it is important that people be involved in fighting injustice. Use examples from Corrie ten Boom's life to illustrate your answer.

3. Betsie ten Boom encouraged Corrie by saying, "Remember, there is no pit so deep that God's love is not deeper" (page 152). Do you think this is true? Give examples from the book to illustrate your answer.

4. Many books and articles have been written about Corrie ten Boom, but she always gave credit to her whole family for their efforts to help the Jews. Explain the roles various family members played in resisting the Nazis. Why do you think Corrie is the family member most often remembered?

5. Corrie wrote, "Worry does not empty tomorrow of its sorrow, it empties today of its strength." Explore this idea with reference to Corrie's own life. How did she learn this lesson, and how did she apply it?

6. After the war, Corrie spoke to others about the need for forgiving one's enemies. Explore the concept of forgiveness. Is it an easy process? Why do you think Corrie felt it was so important to forgive? Whom did Corrie herself need to forgive and for what reasons? How was she able to forgive?

Creative Writing

1. One of the last things Casper ten Boom said to his daughters was "Never forget what a privileged family we are" (page 97). Using examples from the book, write a poem expressing why the Ten Boom family should consider themselves privileged.

2. Read several examples of eulogies and then write an appropriate eulogy for Casper ten Boom.

3. Lieutenant Rahms was obviously very impressed with Corrie and her message. Write an imaginary secret letter from him to his wife explaining his meetings with Corrie and the ways in which Corrie challenged his thinking.

4. Write a newspaper article about a key event in Corrie ten Boom's life. For example, you might report on her success as the leader of the Triangle Club, her qualifying as the first female watchmaker in Holland, or her being taken by the Nazis. Be sure to include a catchy headline.
   [Allocate different events to various students or groups of students and put the articles into a single newspaper format covering Corrie ten Boom's life.]

5. Write a pamphlet that the Dutch underground could have used to recruit and train new members. Include as much information as you can.

6. Pin a Star of David like those that Jewish people were required to wear onto a jacket. Imagining that the jacket belonged to a child in Holland during World War II, write a one-act play featuring the jacket and the child who wore it.

Hands-On Projects

1. Create a mural that represents Holland before, during, and after the war. (You may like to get permission to clip pictures or words from magazines or newspapers to help you.)

2. Draw a map of Holland and Germany. On it label and illustrate the places Corrie ten Boom lived and the events that occurred in her life in those places.

3. Draw a three-circle Venn diagram that shows the similarities and differences in Corrie's life before, during, and after the war.

4. Draw a family crest for the Ten Booms. Incorporate as much information as you can into the crest.

Audio/Visual Projects

1. Write a script that a tour guide could use to give a tour of the Beje. From the script, produce a tape recording of a mock tour, complete with background sounds.

2. The four tenets of the Triangle Club Corrie founded were
   a. Seek your strength through prayer.
   b. Be open and trustworthy.
   c. Bear your difficulties cheerfully.
   d. Develop the gifts that God has given you.

   Write and produce a four-act play (one act for each tenet) that shows how Corrie lived these values out in her own life. Videotape the play.

3. Write and produce a radio play showing how life changed for a Jewish person living in Holland before, during, and after the German invasion.

4. Create a mime to illustrate the following quote, and read the quote as the mime is being performed. Videotape your mime.

   First they came for the communists, and I did not speak up because I was not a communist.

   Then they came for the Jews, and I did not speak up because I was not a Jew.

   Then they came for the Catholics, and I did not speak up because I was a Protestant.

   Then they came for me, and by that time there was no one left.

   Pastor Martin Niemoeller – 1944

5. Create a version of *This Is Your Life* for Corrie ten Boom. Choose key people who would have known her and set up a studio where "Corrie" can meet them again. Videotape your production.

Arts and Crafts

1. One of the jobs given to the women at Ravensbruck was to knit socks for the German troops. Learn some basic knitting stitches and try to knit a square. *[If an entire class does this, the squares could be sewn together to form a blanket. This could be donated to a local charity.]*
2. After the war, many memorials were made to honor the six million Jews and five million others who perished in the Holocaust. Using available materials, such as wood, concrete blocks, cardboard, and plastic containers, make your own memorial to remember some aspect of the Holocaust. Incorporate a plaque into the memorial.
3. Reflect on art about the Holocaust, and create your own picture using watercolors. (To view an art display made by a school group, go to www.remember.org/imagine/index.html)
4. Corrie and her father were clock and watchmakers. Purchase a basic clock movement and hands. (These are available at craft outlets.) Design and illustrate a clock face that reflects some aspect of Dutch life. (This can be done on white paper and laminated for strength.) Assemble the clock.

Language Examples

Below are some examples of sentences written in Dutch. Use them to make banners, posters, and bookmarks, and use them on invitations or place mats for the culminating event.

Jesus is victor.
Jezus is overwinnaar.

God's love shines in the darkness.
De liefde van God shijnt in de duisternis.

This is the victory that overcomes the world, our faith. (1 John 5:4 RSV)
Deze overwinning op de wereld behalen we met ons geloof.

God is Love.
God is liefde.

Thou art my hiding place and my shield. (Psalm 119:114 RSV)
U bent mijn shuilplaats en min schild.

5

Community Links

Many communities have a rich supply of people and places to which students can be exposed to help them learn about and appreciate other cultures. It is well worth the effort to find out what your community has to offer with regard to the unit you are studying. For this unit, for example, you may be able to host a Dutch person or visit a Holocaust memorial.

While it would be wonderful if you could take a field trip to visit some of these people and places, if you can't, it is often possible to have visitors come to the classroom. Whether you decide to take a field trip or invite a guest to your classroom, such activities need to be flanked by sound educational choices. Otherwise, much of the educational value of the event will not be realized. The following three steps will help students derive the greatest educational value from a field trip or classroom visit.

Step One: Preparation

Students should always research the topic before they begin a classroom interview or field trip. In doing so, they will be ready to ask intelligent questions based upon a sound knowledge of their topic. For example, if a Dutch person is coming to visit your class, be sure that the students have a map of the Netherlands on which to pinpoint the area he or she came from.

As the teacher, you need to give the students a clear idea as to why they are going on the field trip and what they are expected to produce with their findings. For example, you might say to them, "We are going to visit a European bakery. When we get back, I want you to be able to sketch, describe, and name five baked items you saw there."

Students should be encouraged to compile lists of questions they want answers to, based upon what they have already learned. They should carry a clipboard with them to write down answers, draw sketches, and note observations. (For less motivated students, a simple worksheet of activities to be completed on the field trip itself can be a good idea.) Such activities reinforce the idea that the field trip is a serious educational event and that the student is there to gather information, not just to be a sightseer.

Step Two: The Event

During the field trip or classroom visit, make sure that the students remain on task. Insist that they be respectful of property and other people at all times. Make sure that you have a spokesperson designated to thank whomever you talk to as well as the parents who help with the event.

Step Three: Processing and Reflection

Students should be given time to process the information they have gathered from their field trip or classroom visit and reflect on it, both individually and as a class. This can take many forms, including making flow charts or diagrams of what they learned, editing interviews for articles or audiovisual presentations, writing reports, and making booklets. Something as simple as a class book called *Did You Know?,* in which each student writes down one fact he or she learned from the field trip, can serve as an effective reflection tool.

Suggested Community Links

Dutch People. Ordinary people are some of the best resources of all. Perhaps there is a Dutch family in your neighborhood. You could invite a member of the family to address the class so that students can learn about the family's history. Did members of the family live under German occupation in the Netherlands? If so, what stories did they pass down? How long has the person or family been in the United States? What part of the Netherlands is the family from? Can the person write or speak something in Dutch for your class? What does the family like to eat at home? What Dutch customs does the family still practice in America?

European or Continental Bakery. Many communities have at least one good Continental bakery or restaurant. Visit the restaurant at a non-busy time (between two and three in the afternoon is normally a good time) and ask the owner if he or she would give your class a demonstration of how a few European foods are cooked and the opportunity to taste some of them. For a small fee, perhaps your class could have a cooking lesson at a time when the restaurant is not busy.

Jewish Synagogue. Contact your nearest Jewish synagogue and, if possible, arrange for your class to visit. Perhaps you could listen to a cantor.

Holocaust Memorial. Contact your nearest Jewish synagogue and speak to someone in public relations. Explain that you are studying a unit that includes the Holocaust and ask the person whether he or she knows of anyone who could speak to the class about it, or where the nearest public display on the Holocaust can be found.

6

Social Studies

The social studies section is divided into three categories, each with suggestions on how to use the material given. The categories are briefly described below.

Places. This section covers significant places related to the story and named in the text of the book *Corrie ten Boom: Keeper of the Angels' Den.*

Geographical Characteristics. This section contains suggestions for mapping some of the physical characteristics of the Netherlands.

Conceptual Questions. This section provides the teacher with conceptual social studies questions related to the book.

Places

These places are categorized by country, with the page number where they are first referred to in the book given in parentheses. Students can undertake a range of activities with these place names. They can

- Locate and mark the places on the relevant country map. (Maps for this purpose are located in the foldout map section in the center of this guide.)
- Note other points, such as their absolute location (latitude and longitude), and then observe how this location compares to other locations mentioned in the book. For example, calculate which location is closer to the equator or the North Pole.
- Calculate the relative locations of various places mentioned in the book. For example, how far is it from Haarlem to Ravensbruck or from the Netherlands across the North Sea to England?
- Construct a key to show population density in the Netherlands.
- Pinpoint the places on a large wall map in the classroom. Students can then use index cards to write explanations as to why the various places are mentioned in the story. Each card could be pinned to the wall with a length of yarn connecting it to the appropriate place on the map.

Places mentioned in the Netherlands

Haarlem (12)
Leiden (21)
Hilversum (34)
Amsterdam (34)
Rotterdam (39)
Velsen (51)
Scheveningen (98)
Vught (136)
Brabant (136)
Groningen (172)

Other locations mentioned

London, England (40)
Paris, France (139)
Ravensbruck, Germany (152)
Berlin, Germany (page 160)
Munich, Germany (191)
Los Angeles, California (199)

Geographical Characteristics

Have students use an atlas to locate the following and then mark them on the blank map of the Netherlands from the foldout map section in the center of this book:

- The Netherlands' two major rivers and their sources and tributaries: the Maas River and the Rhine River with its tributaries the Waal, the IJssel, and the Lek.
- The twelve provinces of the Netherlands.
- Areas of the Netherlands that are below, at, and above sea level.
- The five largest cities in the Netherlands.
- The latitude and longitude lines that bisect the Netherlands.
- The North Sea, IJsselmeer, and the Waddenzee.
- The Netherlands' bordering countries, Belgium and Germany.
- The West Frisian Islands.
- The capital city, Amsterdam, and the seat of government, The Hague.

Conceptual Questions

The following questions are ordered from the simple to the complex. You could ask the students to use these questions to

- Write one or more paragraphs to answer each question.
- Present an oral report to the class on one of the questions.
- Discuss the answer(s) to a question or questions in a group context.

Questions to ponder

1. Locate and name two countries that are larger than the Netherlands, two countries that are about the same size, and two countries that are smaller.
2. How large is the Netherlands compared to the United States? What state is roughly the same size as the Netherlands?
3. How does the population of the Netherlands compare to the population of the United States?
4. Which other major cities lie at about the same latitude as Haarlem?
5. Study a physical map of the Netherlands. Where do you think most of the population would live? Why? Use a population map to test your hypothesis. Were you right or wrong? Why?
6. Using encyclopedias and other resources, trace the history of the Netherlands over the past six hundred years. Which powers have ruled over the Netherlands in that period and for how long?
7. Research the reasons the Netherlands was so strategic to Germany during World War II. What are these reasons?
8. Eight hundred fifty square miles of the Netherlands have been reclaimed from the sea. Research how the Netherlands was able to develop so much land and how it keeps it dry.

7

Related Themes to Explore

Any unit study has natural links to many other topics that can also be explored. While it is impossible to pursue all such links in this context, the spoke diagram on the next page shows some related topics that students might find interesting to study alongside Corrie ten Boom.

There are two ways you might like to integrate some of these links into your classroom. Some teachers and parents have the flexibility to be able to choose the topics their students study and even to alter their selections partway through the year. If you are able to do this, use the theme wheel to help identify other topics you might like to follow up this unit with. For example, after studying Corrie ten Boom, your students might become interested in the history and current status of the Dutch royal family or the current attempts to find out what happened to the millions of dollars that belonged to Jews in Europe before World War II. If you are studying statistics in math, there is a wealth of statistics about World War II that could be converted into pie, line, bar, and pictographs.

Other teachers and parents are locked in to a less flexible curriculum. If this is your situation, you may still have the ability to change the order in which various topics are taught. Look through the topics listed to see whether any coincide with topics you have already scheduled for later in the year. Consider the possibility of scheduling the teaching of these topics closer to this unit so that cross-curriculum learning can take place.

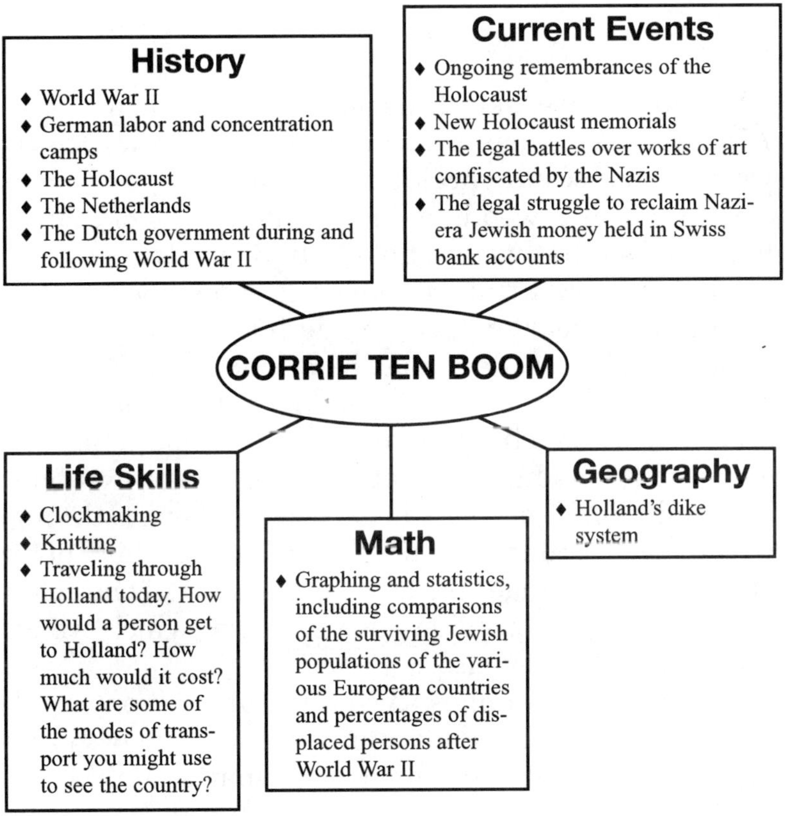

CORRIE TEN BOOM

History
- World War II
- German labor and concentration camps
- The Holocaust
- The Netherlands
- The Dutch government during and following World War II

Current Events
- Ongoing remembrances of the Holocaust
- New Holocaust memorials
- The legal battles over works of art confiscated by the Nazis
- The legal struggle to reclaim Nazi-era Jewish money held in Swiss bank accounts

Life Skills
- Clockmaking
- Knitting
- Traveling through Holland today. How would a person get to Holland? How much would it cost? What are some of the modes of transport you might use to see the country?

Math
- Graphing and statistics, including comparisons of the surviving Jewish populations of the various European countries and percentages of displaced persons after World War II

Geography
- Holland's dike system

8

Culminating Event

As adults, we like to have a reason to learn something. We learn a new computer program so that we can balance our checking account, a song so that we can sing it at a wedding, or the rudiments of another language so that we are able to find our way around a foreign country. Students have the same need for purpose in their learning. It is valid but not very motivational to tell a student that he or she needs to gather and learn information to pass a test or move up a grade. It is much more motivational for a student when he or she has some other, more meaningful goal in mind. This goal can be a specific forum through which each student can express his or her newly acquired knowledge. We believe that part of the role of the teacher is to provide such a forum, which we call the culminating event.

As the name implies, the culminating event marks the end of the unit study and gives a sense of closure to the topic. It also serves to put what students have learned into a larger context that can then be shared with others.

The culminating event can be as simple as inviting the class next door (or the homeschooled children down the street) to come and hear poems and stories and view the written work that students have completed. Conversely, it could be as involved as hosting a parent/neighborhood dinner featuring Dutch food, songs, and games along with plays and presentations on the life and achievements of Corrie ten Boom.

No matter how simple or elaborate the culminating event is, make sure you have the broad outline of it in mind before planning the other activities for your unit study, as the two are integrally linked.

Idea Sparks

Food: Prepare and serve Dutch food. The Dutch tend to eat simple, nutritious food. Lunch normally consists of a range of the following: salad, cold meat, bread, cheese (a variety of types, including Gouda and Edam), hard-boiled eggs, and coffee. Dinner often consists of one of the following: thick soup and bread; *boerenomelet,* an omelet stuffed with potato, meat, and vegetables; *boerenkool met rookwurst,* a kale and potato dish eaten with mixed vegetables; *klapstuk,* beef stew; and *pannekoeken,* pancakes served with syrup or bacon.

Music: Play classical music or the Dutch national anthem in the background to set the mood. (Many libraries stock music selections. The anthem has fifteen verses, but normally only the first and sixth are sung.)

Flowers: The Dutch love bunches of fresh flowers. They use them to celebrate just about any occasion. You might like to use some as a centerpiece if you prepare a Dutch meal.

Oral Presentations. Present poems, essays, reports, speeches, reviews, and devotions that students have written during the course of the unit study.

Display. Display other work, including artwork, map work, models, newspapers, and video interviews.

Appendix A

Books and Resources

This appendix is divided into seven sections: (1) other biographies of Corrie ten Boom, (2) books written by Corrie ten Boom, (3) related books, (4) related movies and documentaries, (5) related articles from *National Geographic,* (6) Internet sites, and (7) other resources.

There are over two hundred books either written by Corrie ten Boom or written about her. It is impossible to list them all here, but the teacher could go online and locate the full list in an online bookstore.

Many books about Corrie ten Boom are written at a higher reading level than the books in the Christian Heroes: Then & Now series and would be interesting for a teacher to read for his or her own information and as background for the unit. Children learn best by example, so consider choosing one good adult book to read and enrich your own understanding of the topic. Resources for younger readers are also included if they can be found, making it easy for younger family members or less able readers to participate in the unit study at their own level.

Some of the books listed here are more difficult to get copies of than others. If they are not available at your local Christian bookstore, many of the titles can be located in secondhand bookstores (try using the Internet to locate them). Most are also available through the national interlibrary loan service.

Other Biographies of Corrie ten Boom

All the biographies listed on the bibliography page of *Corrie ten Boom: Keeper of the Angels' Den,* as well as others that may be of interest, are listed here. Each listing has basic information on how to locate the book. The approximate age level of the intended reader is also given, along with the number of pages in each book and some comments to help you decide whether you might want to include this book in your unit study.

TITLE: *The Secret Room*
Author: David Wallington
Publisher: Chansitor Press
Age Level: Grades 2–3, 6,500 words

Synopsis: This easily understood text covers Corrie's life in a simple and undisturbing manner.

Comments: While this book is no longer in print, it can be downloaded free of charge at www.soon.org.uk/true_stories/holocaust.htm. Excellent questions have also been written to accompany the text.

TITLE: *Corrie ten Boom: Heroine of Haarlem*
Author: Sam Wellman

Publisher: Barbour, 1995
ISBN: 1557487294
Age Level: Easy Adult, 208 pages

Synopsis: This book covers all of Corrie's life but gives special attention to her childhood.

Comments: This book tends to be a little preachy in places, which may make it less appealing to younger readers. However, it does contain some good information.

TITLE: *Corrie ten Boom*
Author: Kathleen White
Publisher: Bethany House, 1991
ISBN: 1556611943
Age Level: Adult, 112 pages

Synopsis: This book tells Corrie ten Boom's life story, paying particular attention to details of the Ten Boom family history and how the family has been entwined with Jewish people for several generations.

Comments: This story is not told sequentially and tends to be a little preachy at times.

TITLE: *Corrie ten Boom*
Author: Barbera Nooitgedagt
Publisher: Child Evangelism Fellowship
ISBN: 155976600X
Age Level: Young Child

Synopsis: This is not a traditional book but a series of five full-color flashcard lessons based on the life of Corrie ten Boom.

Comments: While this series will be too young for most readers, younger children can use it to study the same topic, or older children might like to practice the flashcard lessons and teach them to a younger audience. Alternately, you might like to use the flashcards to spark students' ideas for writing related poems, letters, or newspaper articles. These could then be displayed as a consecutive representation of Corrie's life. This flashcard series can be ordered directly from Child Evangelism Fellowship at 1-800-748-7710.

Books Written by Corrie ten Boom

Four books, three of them written by Corrie, give a detailed account of her life from birth to death when read together. These books are *In My Father's House* (covering her life before World War II), *The Hiding Place* (relating her life during the war), *Tramp for the Lord* (recounting her adventures after the war), and *The Five Silent Years of Corrie ten Boom* (looking at the last five years of Corrie's life). This last book is listed in the Related Books section.

TITLE: *In My Father's House: The Years Before the Hiding Place*
Author: Corrie ten Boom with Carole C. Carlson
Publisher: Fleming H. Revell, 2000
ISBN: 0800717716
Age Level: Adult, 272 pages

Synopsis: In this book, Corrie recounts her life before World War II.

TITLE: *The Hiding Place*
Author: Corrie ten Boom with John and Elizabeth Sherrill
Publisher: Bantam Books, 1984
ISBN: 0553256696
Age Level: Adult, 256 pages

Synopsis: This book covers Corrie's childhood quickly and then goes on to focus on her life during World War II, especially her underground activities and imprisonment in Ravensbruck.

Comments: This well-written Christian classic is fast paced yet pays close attention to the many details of Corrie's life.

TITLE: *Corrie Ten Boom's Prison Letters*
Publisher: Fleming H. Revell, 1975
ISBN: 0800707397
Age Level: Adult, 90 pages

Synopsis: This is a collection of letters written by Corrie from prison.

TITLE: *Tramp for the Lord*
Author: Corrie ten Boom with Jamie Buckingham
Publisher: Fleming H. Revell, 1998
ISBN: 0800717570
Age Level: Adult, 288 pages

Synopsis: This book recounts Corrie's international adventures as a Christian speaker after the war.

Related Books

This section contains a list of other books that fit around the life story of Corrie ten Boom. ISBN numbers, age level, and relevant comments are included for each book listed. The books are organized into two subsections, nonfiction and fiction.

Of course, there are many other books that relate in some way to this topic. You may want to record inside the back cover of this unit study guide the titles of other books you find particularly helpful.

Nonfiction

TITLE: *The Five Silent Years of Corrie ten Boom*
Author: Pamela Rosewell Moore
Publisher: Zondervan, 1986
ISBN: 0310611210
Age Level: Adult, 256 pages

Synopsis: This is an intimate account of the last five years of Corrie ten Boom's life after she suffered a serious stroke.

Comments: Obviously this book is reflective and lacks the action of the books that recount Corrie's earlier life. However, it does give insight into Corrie's final years.

TITLE: *Return to the Hiding Place*
Author: Hans Poley
Publisher: Chariot Victor, 1993
ISBN: 0781409322
Age Level: Adult, 224 pages

Synopsis: This is a first-person account of the war years in Holland told by Hans Poley, who was himself a "guest" at the Beje.

Comments: This is a great book to accompany a unit on Corrie ten Boom. Poley relates a lot of interesting information and impressions of Corrie and her family. The book also contains photographs.

TITLE: *The Holocaust: A History of Courage and Resistance*
Author: Bea Stadtler
Publisher: Behrman House, 1995
ISBN: 0874415780
Age Level: Grades 4–8, 197 pages

Synopsis: This is a clearly written account of the events leading up to and during World War II as they pertain to the fate of European Jews and others deemed "undesirable."

Comments: This very informative book is considered by many to be the most readable textbook on the Holocaust for grades 4–8. Each chapter ends with questions to think about, and there is also a thorough and thoughtful accompanying discussion guide written by Nancy Karkowsky.

The following true stories also deal with the Nazi atrocities during World War II and people's struggles to overcome them.

TITLE: *Hilde and Eli: Children of the Holocaust*
Author: David A. Adler
Publisher: Holiday House, 1994
ISBN: 0823410919
Age Level: Elementary school, 32 pages

Synopsis: This picture book is set in Germany.

TITLE: *Clara's Story*
Author: Clara Isaacman and Joan Adess Grossman
Publisher: Jewish Publication Society of America, 1984
ISBN: 0827605064
Age Level: Middle school, 180 pages

Synopsis: This story is set in Belgium.

TITLE: *The Upstairs Room*
Author: Johanna Reiss
Publisher: HarperCollins, 1990
ISBN: 006440370X
Age Level: Middle school, 208 pages

Synopsis: This story is set in Holland.

TITLE: *Anne Frank: The Diary of a Young Girl*
Author: Anne Frank
Publisher: Bantam, 1993
ISBN: 0553296981
Age Level: Middle school, 304 pages

Synopsis: This story is set in Holland.

TITLE: *Struggle: The True Story of a Teenager Who Fought to Stay Alive*
Author: Sara Zyskind
Publisher: Lerner Publishing, 1989
ISBN: 822507722
Age Level: High school, 288 pages

Synopsis: This story is set in Poland.

Fiction

A number of wonderful fiction books on this topic are available for young people. Students may enjoy reading one or more of these books alongside *Corrie ten Boom: Keeper of the Angels' Den.*

TITLE: *The Lily Cupboard: A Story of the Holocaust*
Author: Shulamith Levey Oppenheim
Publisher: HarperCollins, 1995
ISBN: 0064433935
Age Level: Elementary school, 32 pages

Comments: This story is set in Holland.

TITLE: *Number the Stars*
Author: Lois Lowry
Publisher: Bantam Doubleday Dell, 1990
ISBN: 0440403278

Age Level: Grades 3–5, 144 pages

Comments: This story is set in Denmark.

TITLE: *Hide and Seek*
Author: Ida Vos
Publisher: Penguin Putnam, 1995
ISBN: 0140369082
Age Level: Middle school, 144 pages

Comments: This story is set in Holland.

TITLE: *The Devil's Arithmetic*
Author: Jane Yolen
Publisher: Penguin Putnam, 1990
ISBN: 0140345353
Age Level: Middle school, 170 pages

Comments: This story is set in Poland. There is a video based on this story.

Related Movies and Documentaries

Listed in this section are movies and documentaries that have been made about the life of Corrie ten Boom or issues and/or people who have some relationship to events in her life. The rating for each movie or documentary is included when available, but as with all unfamiliar material, it is prudent to preview them before showing them to students.

Movies and documentaries are particularly useful in showing the visual details of another place and time period. As students watch, encourage them to study the clothing, weather, crops, terrain, and other geographical factors shown in the movie or documentary.

TITLE: *The Hiding Place*
Director: James F. Collier
Type: True drama
Length: 145 minutes
Rated: PG

Comments: This movie closely follows the story line of the book *The Hiding Place*. It is well worth showing to a class.

TITLE: *The Charm of Holland*
Director: Sherilyn Mentes
Type: Travelog
Length: 60 minutes
ISBN: 093893919X
Rated: N/A

Comments: This is a great video introducing Holland and its history, battle with the sea, and modern life. It is no longer available for purchase, but it may be available for loan at your local library.

TITLE: *Holland, Luxembourg, Belgium*
Director: N/A
Type: Travelog
Length: 70 minutes
ISBN: 1563450739
Rated: N/A

Comments: This is also a very good general introduction to Dutch life, past and present. It has brief clips of Haarlem. It also has a brief glimpse of the Red Light District, which you will want to preview, although there is nothing explicit.

TITLE: *Survivors of the Holocaust*
Director: Allan Holzman
Type: Documentary

Length: 70 minutes
ISBN: 9780611926
Rated: N/A

Comments: This outstanding documentary includes interviews and artwork of survivors of the Holocaust. It is very moving, but the speakers talk matter-of-factly for the most part. There is one picture of nude female prisoners and one shot of dead bodies being loaded into a cart, but these do not stand out in the tragic context of the documentary.

TITLE: *Looking into the Face of Evil*
Director: Sam Nahem
Type: Documentary
Length: 28 minutes
Rated: N/A

Comments: This is a brief history of the Jews in Europe during World War II as seen through the eyes of three survivors and one American soldier who helped liberate a concentration camp. It is particularly good at showing the progression of alienation that the Jews were subjected to. It has some actual footage that includes piles of dead nude bodies, but again within the context of the discussion these are appropriate photographs. You may want to edit out the last interview with the soldier as he gives a graphic account of Nazi experiments on human remains.

TITLE: *Schindler's List*
Director: Steven Spielberg
Type: Drama
Length: 197 minutes
Rated: R

Comments: This stark movie shows how the Jewish people in Europe were slowly marginalized and then disposed of.

Unfortunately, it has explicit sex scenes along with nudity and extreme violence. Because it is such a well-known movie, you may wish to show appropriate excerpts to your students after carefully previewing it. (If you are a schoolteacher you need to be very careful that parents give permission and understand that their children are watching an edited version.)

TITLE: *"Two Couples" Rescuers: Stories of Courage*
Directors: Lynne Littman and Tim Hunter
Type: True drama
Length: 109 minutes
ISBN: 6305099057
Rated: PG

Comments: This is an excellent dramatization of the true stories of two couples. The first story is set in Holland, where a newlywed couple hide up to thirty-five Jewish people at a time in their country home. The second story deals with a childless Flemish couple who are ordered to run a local Catholic boys boarding school. The couple slowly become involved in the resistance movement and end up fostering many Jewish boys in plain sight. (To understand the second story, students would have to be familiar with the practice of circumcision and the fact that Jewish boys looked different from non-Jewish boys.) These stories are very well acted, and the first one in particular deals with many of the same problems Corrie encountered.

[Note: There are two other videos in this series, "Two Women" and "Two Families." These four stories contain some inappropriate language, but nonetheless they are very well crafted vignettes of life under Nazi occupation.]

Related *National Geographic* Articles

Many magazines contain articles related to this unit study. We have chosen to reference *National Geographic* because it can provide contemporaneous commentary on many events, since it dates back to the 1880s, and because it is widely available in libraries and schools throughout the country.

These articles and their accompanying photographs represent just some of those available that bear on aspects of Corrie ten Boom's life. They can be used in a variety of ways to support and reinforce this unit study. For example, you could have students analyze the article "Holland Rises from War and Water" (February 1946), which describes Holland during liberation. Students could make a chart comparing Corrie's experiences when she was released to the conditions mentioned in the article. A student could also select a photograph from "Low Countries Await Liberation" (August 1944) and write a poem about it through the eyes of a Dutch citizen. The poem could be displayed with the photograph.

Articles about Holland contemporaneous with Corrie

TITLE: As Seen from a Dutch Window
Issue Date: September 1908, pages 619–634

Description: A rambling but informative account of everything from Dutch window washers to Dutch houses and the national habit of cigar smoking.

TITLE: Glimpses of Holland
Issue Date: January 1915, pages 1–29

Description: A look at Holland, its canal system, culture, and ongoing struggle against the sea.

TITLE: A Vacation in Holland
Issue Date: September 1929, pages 363–378

Description: The author and his family vacation at the seaside and visit many places in Holland, including Haarlem.

TITLE: Low Countries Await Liberation
Issue Date: August 1944, pages 221–228

Description: A photo spread of scenes from German-occupied Belgium and the Netherlands. Contains excellent photos of bombed-out Rotterdam.

TITLE: Holland Rises from War and Water
Issue Date: February 1946, pages 237–260

Description: This article presents Holland during and immediately after liberation by the Allies. There are photos of U.S. food drops, cities flooded from dike damage, and liberated children. The article offers an excellent context in which to view Corrie's return to her homeland.

Another article of interest

TITLE: Remnants: The Last Jews of Poland
Issue Date: September 1986, pages 362–389

Description: This very moving story traces the fates of Polish Jews who survived the Holocaust.

Internet Sites

The websites listed here may have been updated since this guide was published and as a result may contain information not reviewed here. Because of this, it is vital that you preview the sites before allowing your students to view them. General websites about the Netherlands will likely mention the Red Light District of Amsterdam and the Dutch government's permissive attitude toward drug use. Likewise, websites about the Holocaust may well contain pictures of the killing and incinerating of people.

Websites related to Corrie ten Boom

www.amadeus-hotel.com

This site has excellent tourist information on Haarlem, including a map of the city showing the Beje (site of the Corrie ten Boom Museum), St. Bavo Church, and other important landmarks. The site also has a Corrie ten Boom Museum page, which gives a synopsis of Corrie's story.

www.corrietenboom.com

This site is a good introduction to Corrie's life. It includes photos of the Beje along with a range of family photos.

Websites about Holland

www.soon.org.uk/country/netherlands.htm

This general information site on the Netherlands includes tourist information, Dutch language samples (including the *Four Spiritual Laws*), and a link to the Anne Frank House.

www.xs4all.nl/~bslikker/start.html

This Dutch music site includes the words and tune of the Dutch national anthem.

www.graphicsbycarla.com/folklore.htm

This well-constructed site features Dutch culture, habits, recipes, national costumes, and the like.

Holocaust-related websites

www.ushmm.org

This is the official site of the United States Holocaust Memorial Museum in Washington, D.C. It contains everything you could want to know about the museum as well as online exhibits, document and photo archives, and dates for Holocaust Remembrance Day.

www.historyplace.com/index.html

Scroll down to Nazi Germany/World War II for a wonderful site with extensive information on World War II, including a biography of Adolf Hitler, an examination of the Hitler Youth Movement, and a detailed timeline of World War II and Holocaust events.

www.remember.org

This is a huge "cybrary" on the Holocaust containing numerous resources, including photos, poems, concentration camp maps, memoirs, an online bookstore, lesson plans, and lots more.

www.holocaustbooks.org

This is the online bookstore of the United States Holocaust Memorial Museum. It has a comprehensive range of books on the Holocaust and genocide, as well as videos, music, and teaching materials.

www.hwrc.org

Click on Resources, then History + Documents for a huge

range of World War II documents and audio recordings. Under History + Documents, click on Forgotten Camps to find information on Ravensbruck, including photographs, maps, and history.

Other Resources

TITLE: *The Holocaust*
Publisher: Scholastic

Synopsis: Scholastic produces a single-issue children's magazine titled *The Holocaust.* This twenty-four-page color and black-and-white magazine includes maps, photos, survivors' stories, a play, and general information. Order by calling Scholastic at 1-800-724-6527.

TITLE: *Learning about the Holocaust: Literature and Other Resources for Young People*
Authors: Elaine C. Stephens, Jean E. Brown, and Janet E. Rubin
Publisher: Library Professional Publications, 1995
ISBN: 0208024085

Synopsis: This 198-page book is a definitive guide to Holocaust resources and where they can be purchased. Categories include background material, informational books, photo essays, maps, personal narratives, poetry, historical fiction, plays, organizations and institutions, curriculum guides, films, videos, and audio recordings.

Appendix B

Answers to Chapter Questions

Chapter One

1. A curfew is a time after which people must be indoors for the night.
2. The Gestapo took Corrie and her family to a gymnasium at the Haarlem police headquarters.
3. Corrie was worried that the Gestapo might learn that six people were hidden in a secret room in the Beje.

Chapter Two

1. A disorder is a disturbance of the normal working of the body.
2. Corrie had appendicitis.
3. Corrie decided to become a watchmaker because wristwatches were becoming more common and her father needed someone in the clockshop who was trained to make and repair them.

Chapter Three

1. Assurance is complete confidence in the way something is going to turn out.
2. The Ten Booms had two radios at the Beje before the war.
3. Peter thought the stairway would be a good place to hide a radio because the radio could be hidden in a hollow under the planks and because the nearby piano could be played to drown out its sound.

Chapter Four

1. Allies are countries that have agreed to be on the same side of a conflict.
2. The Germans required all Jews to wear a patch bearing a yellow Star of David with “Jew” stamped across it.
3. Willem suggested that Corrie steal ration cards for the Jewish guests.

Chapter Five

1. A cantor is the person who leads the musical part of a service at a church or synagogue.
2. Corrie used her tire-less bicycle to get around Haarlem.
3. Mr. Smit thought the Beje was an ideal house in which to make a secret room because it had so many irregular angles and floor levels.

Chapter Six

1. A dynamo is a machine that converts mechanical energy into electric energy.

2. Eusie began singing a birthday song to Mr. Ten Boom.
3. Corrie let Jop leave the Beje because he volunteered to warn another underground house that it was going to be raided and there wasn't time to ask an underground worker to take the message.

Chapter Seven

1. Defiantly means with an attitude of deliberate resistance of something or someone, especially someone in authority.
2. Peter was imprisoned for two weeks and warned never to play the anthem again.
3. The Gestapo officer was delighted when there was a knock at the Beje door because he thought it would be someone else associated with the underground movement whom he could capture.

Chapter Eight

1. Recoiled means to have suddenly drawn back in disgust, horror, or alarm.
2. Corrie dropped her watch and her mother's wedding ring into the manila envelope.
3. The young baroness was in prison because her father had refused to serve in the German navy.

Chapter Nine

1. Pleurisy is an inflammation of the chest and lung membranes.
2. Two bars of soap, a chain of safety pins, and four Gospel booklets were in the package the nurse gave to Corrie.

3. The prisoners were able to yell messages to one another because the guards all went to a party to celebrate Hitler's birthday.

Chapter Ten

1. Defective means faulty or imperfect.
2. Lieutenant Rahms interviewed Corrie.
3. The lieutenant tried to get Corrie to talk by treating her kindly, hoping she would be fooled into thinking she had found a friend in the Gestapo.

Chapter Eleven

1. An emblem is a design or object that represents, or symbolizes, something else.
2. The new camp was called Vught.
3. The prisoners got their information about the progress of the war from new prisoners who came into the camp.

Chapter Twelve

1. Auburn is a reddish-brown color.
2. Eighty women were forced into each boxcar.
3. The seven teenage boys were able to control the women because they had guns and because the women were too weak to resist them.

Chapter Thirteen

1. Clamored means to have raised a noisy outcry.
2. Corrie and Betsie worked at the Siemens factory.
3. Corrie was thankful because the guards would not come into the barracks because of the fleas, leaving Corrie and Betsie free to hold Bible studies and prayer meetings without being caught.

Chapter Fourteen

1. Scrawny means overly skinny or thin.
2. Corrie was driven in a limousine.
3. Nurse Benes did not recognize Corrie because Corrie looked so old.

Chapter Fifteen

1. Palatial means extremely large or splendid, like a palace.
2. Corrie visited more than sixty countries after the war.
3. Corrie refused to have schedules and bells because she did not want to create an atmosphere that would remind the guests of the Nazis.